Richard C. Adams

A Delaware Indian Legend and the Story of their Troubles

Richard C. Adams

A Delaware Indian Legend and the Story of their Troubles

ISBN/EAN: 9783337153632

Printed in Europe, USA, Canada, Australia, Japan

Cover: Foto ©ninafisch / pixelio.de

More available books at **www.hansebooks.com**

Yours Sincerely
Richard C. Adams.

TO THE AMERICAN PEOPLE.

WITH your kind permission, your attention I will claim,
    I am only just an Indian, it matters not my name,
But I represent my people, their cause and interest, too :
And in their name and honor, I present myself to you.
They have your sacred promise, your pledge of friendship warm,
That you would always aid them and protect them from all harm,
And in my humble efforts, as I briefly state their case,
Will you pardon my shortcomings, and my errors all erase?

I do not come with grandeur, or boast of any fame,
Rank in politics, society, or wealth I cannot claim,
I never went to college, have no title of LL. D.,
As the Great Spirit made me, is all that you may see.
With the forces that oppose me, I certainly should pause,
If I were not depending on the justice of my cause.
I am only just an Indian, who here represents his band ;
With this simple introduction, I extend to you my hand.

A DELAWARE INDIAN LEGEND.

L ONG, long ago, my people say, as their traditions tell,
   They were a happy, powerful race, loved and respected well.
To them belonged the sacred charge, the synagogue ([1]) to keep,
And every Autumn to the tribes, the Manitou's praises speak.
And all things went with them full well, the Manitou was pleased;
The Indian race was numerous then, countless as the trees;
The Maniton was kind to them, he filled the woods with game,
And in the rivers and the seas were fish of every name.

And to his children did he give the vast and broad domain;
Some the mountains and valleys took, while others chose the plain :
And everything to comfort them did the Manitou provide,
He gave them fish, game, herbs and maize, and other things beside.
He gave them rivers, lakes and bays, o'er which canoes did glide,
Forests dense and mountains high, great plains the other side.
The men were strong and brave and true, to them belonged the chase,
The women loving, kind and good, who filled a simpler place.

And they were taught while here on earth their spirits to prepare,
To join the Manitou himself, in the happy hunting-ground ([2]) somewhere :
That they must never lie and steal ; must for each other care ;
That principles are gems that pass us to that country there.
And even though the wars do come with aggressive tribe or band,
No warrior shall strike a fallen foe, or wrong a helpless hand ;
And if your foe shall sue for peace, let not his plea be vain,
Produce the pipe, and smoke with him, smothering the wrathful flame.

And while the smoke ascends above, breathe a prayer together,
That spirits of departed friends make peace beyond the river ;
The Maniton's compassion seek, for he was sorely grieved,
Provide for the widows of the slain, ([3]) that their needs be relieved.
If a stranger enters in your lodge, give him both food and bed,
E'en if known to be your foe, no harm hangs o'er his head,
For now he is your honored guest, your protection he does claim ;
Whate'er your source of difference be, contest it on the plain.

The voice of the Great Spirit now is heard in every clime,
The rumblings of the thunder, the whisperings of the pine ;
The works of the Great Spirit are seen on every hand,
Flowers, forests, mountains, stars, sun and even man.
The Lenape (¹) all should gather in the Autumn there to praise
The wonders of the Manitou, the goodness of his grace ;
And they to tell the Nations what to them he has unbound,
And the way for them to reach the happy hunting-ground.

Once many thousand moons ago, in the synagogue there came
All the tribes and warriors from the forest, hill and plain ;
And while they were assembled there (⁵) a young man rose to say,
The Manitou had shown him in a vision on that day
From afar a huge canoe with pinions spreading wide,
Coming o'er the waters from across the sunrise side ;
And in that huge canoe were people strange of dress,
All were armed as warriors, though they peacefulness professed.

They told them of their God, " who came and died for men,"
And they were messengers from Him to save them from their sin,
But first, they said, they must have land, and thus a home prepare,
Then they would teach them truth, and heaven with them share.
The young man to the warriors old his vision further told,
And prophesied that from that day these tempters would grow bold ;
That each would have a different creed, to teach a different tribe,
And when one told another each would think the other lied.

The young man for his people lamented loud and long ;
He saw the friendship broken that always had been strong,
Dissension, war, and trouble, their happiness succeed,
Tribes rise against each other, their warriors die and bleed.
At last, their faith all shattered, home, game and country gone.
Dejected, broken-hearted, he saw them westward roam.
The Manitou was sorrowful that they should faithless (⁶) be,
"And now where is the heaven the stranger promised thee ? "

And some of the young warriors did live to see the day,
When across the sea from sunrise, with pinions flying gay,
Came great canoes with strangers who soon did boldly land,
And with a friendly gesture, extended the right hand.
Forgetful of the warning, they received them all as friends :
And made the sacred pledges to share with them their lands.
The Indians, true and faithful, their promise did fulfill,
And eager sought the teachings of the white man's God and will.

And this recalls sweet memories of at least one truthful man ;
He made and kept a promise in treating for our land ;
His deeds of loving-kindness strength to their teachings lend,
And sacred in our memory is the name of William Penn.
But alas! for faith and trusting, few others like him came,
The white man's promised friendship, thenceforth we found was vain.
While noble were his teachings, his practice was deceit, (⁷)
And thus the friends we trusted, our fondest hopes defeat.

And now the road is open across the stormy sea,
The strangers are invaders—our friends no longer be!
Our Manitou is angry, their God hears not our cry,
On the bloody field of battle the noble warriors die.
Again with peace and presents our friendship would be sought, (⁸)
Requesting that our vengeance on some other tribe be brought.
And now for this protection and their proffered friendship-hand,
The boasted Christian strangers ask to have as much more land. (⁹)

Now many moons have passed, the Indians are but few ;
For comments on the prophecy, I'll leave that all to you.
Is the white man still deceiving? Is the Indian being robbed?
Will he yet share his heaven and the teachings of his God?
The Indian was just a savage, but he would not lie and steal,
The white man's highly civilized, but his conscience could not feel,
To rob poor, trusting Indians—well, to him it was no sin,
And to break a solemn treaty was a very clever thing.

And when the Indian to the white man makes complaint about his land,
He is told with solemn gestures, "Seek the Government—not the man."
" He will be your good, great father and adopt you as his child,
He knows better what you need, and will protect you all the while."
But the father was forgetful (¹⁰) of his foster children's care,
So the Indian thus discouraged, finds relief not anywhere.
Will a Nation for its actions have to pass the judgment bar,
Or will God excuse the people, if the deeds the Nation's are?

He now sees the " Good, Great Father," better known as " Uncle Sam,"
Offering home, aid and protection to the poor of foreign lands ;
Sees the foreigners in numbers seek his own beloved shore,
Where justice, love and liberty reign free forever more.
Sees the foreigners in Council, aid in making laws most just,
While he's no voice in legislation and his lands are held in trust.
Do you know a greater torture, or think his feelings can be guessed
When he sees such freedom cherished, while his own rights are oppressed?

When on the day of judgment, their records there to see,
As God turns o'er the pages, who will the braver be?
For one is just a savage, his simple faith applies ;
The other one, a white man, very highly civilized.
And should they be together long enough to treat,
Do you suppose the white man the Indian there would cheat?
Or if the chance is given, when the judgment's handed down,
Would the white man take his heaven or the Indians' Hunting-Ground?

Do you think that Missionaries need be sent to foreign land,
To find fields for Christian duties and neglect the savage man?
In the land of peace and freedom can bondmen still be found?
Where every man does loudly boast class-legislation is not known!
Should neither one sit on the jury without the aid of ex-parte law,
Were the records brought from heaven, the court hear what the angels saw,
Have you doubts about the judgment? Would the white man pay the cost?
Or would the heir by birthright learn that there his case was lost?

In this the Indian's version, can he still be justified,
Or was it for his poor sake, too, that Christ was crucified?
Will Christians stand by idly, nor lend a helping hand,
And by their silence justify the seizure of his land?
Or will their God from heaven hear the Indian's plea
And prompt the Christian people to lend him sympathy,
And through their earnest efforts, not sympathy alone,
Redeem the Nation's credit before the Judgment Throne?

Let the Indian have some duties, treat him as a worthy man,
Give him voice in the elections, give him title to his land,
Give him place of trust and honor, let him feel this yet his home,
Let him use his mind and muscle, let his actions be his own,
Pay him what is justly due him, let your Government be his, too,
He will battle with each problem, just as faithfully as you.
One who proves himself a warrior and of danger knows no fear,
Surely can find ways to master each new problem that draws near.

NOTE 1. The Delaware Indians on the full moon of each October have
a religious meeting in a large, long building, which lasts twelve days. Here
the clans of the Delawares gather and other Indian tribes are invited. The
ceremonies are conducted in the way of a dance around a fire built in the
centre of the building. At these meetings any brave or chief may tell his
experience in hunting or warfare, his dreams or impressions, and give his
own interpretation of the same, never claiming any of the honors himself if
he has been successful in any event, but thanking the Great Spirit or Manitou

for his success. They believe that every person has a guardian spirit whose duty is to watch and prompt him in his daily actions, and if the individual listens to his guardian spirit he will not meet with any mishap or danger.

NOTE 2. The North American Indian, and especially the Algonquins, of whom the Delawares were the head, is perhaps the most religious being on the face of the earth. While he was warlike and always ready to assert his rights, he was always fearful of angering the Great Spirit, and careful to follow the principles of his traditional teachings, and if it had not been for this sentiment, I do not believe the Indians would ever have allowed the white man to secure a foot-hold on this continent.

NOTE 3. One of the principles of Indian warfare, when peace was made, was to send men from one tribe to the other where the most warriors had been slain, who would provide game for their widows, at least for a certain length of time.

NOTE 4. Some of the Delaware Indians still keep up the old traditionary worship, and on their reservation in the Cherokee Nation, on the forks of Caney, may be seen one of their synagogues, where each October they gather to praise the Great Spirit as their ancestors had taught.

NOTE 5.—I have heard many old men of the Delaware tribe of Indians refer to this prophecy.

NOTE 6.—Some of the Delawares to this day fully believe that their troubles are attributable to the fact of the Indians deserting the form of worship their ancestors had taught and taking up the white man's religion.

NOTE 7.—I quote from the address delivered by Hon. Herbert Welsh before the Society of the Indian Rights Association, April 9, 1892.

The Indian version of this matter is even more pathetic than this account :

"Zeisberger's Christian Indians communities were the admiration of all who visited them. They shone as gleams of sunlight amid the sombre forests of Pennsylvania. Indians, who, but a short time before had been wild and revengeful men, became, under the preaching and indefatigable labors of Zeisberger, peaceable and industrious. They felled the great trees, cultivated the soil; built dwellings and Mission Chapels, and settled into peaceful and as they thought, permanent communities. But they were from the first regarded with envy and suspicion by the rougher elements in the rough and unrestrained colonial population. Ravaging war parties, composed of French officers and savage Indians, devastated the frontier settlements during the French and Indian war, and naturally there arose in undiscriminating and ignorant minds an intense hatred of all Indians. The Moravian Missionaries and their followers were obliged to fly for the protection of the British garrison in Philadelphia to find a shelter, which was grudgingly and timidly given. But a momentary respite was obtained. New York was asked the privilege of an asylum for the Moravian Indians, but the request was refused. A year of heart-sick wandering and exile ensued. The Indians were finally permitted to make the futile attempt of creating new homes for themselves in their native regions. When the storm of the Revolution broke, they were again subjected to the same persecutions as before, culminating in the shameful tragedy known as the Massacre of Gnadenhutten, where ninety of their men, women and children fell unresisting victims beneath the mallets and scalping knives of American Rangers. The Moravian Missions never fairly rallied from this blow. Zeisberger, one of the noblest and most Christian of men, died at Goshen, on the shores of the Tuscanawas, at a great age. Strong in the testimony of a good conscience, but with the harvest of his life's work lying waste about his dying eyes, he gazed sadly on the remnant of his Indian followers who gathered to bid him farewell. From the standpoint of worldly success, his life had been in vain, but not as viewed from the higher standpoint, for he had brought hundreds not only to the conception of a noble life, but to such living of it as put the behaviour of their enemies to shame."

I also refer you to the massacre in Ohio at the Jesuit Mission in 1781 where more than one hundred Christian Indians were killed and burned, mostly women and children, by the American soldiers.

NOTE 8. The first treaty the United States ever made was made with the Delaware Indians, and the greater portion of the Delawares assisted the United States in the Revolutionary war ; also in the Civil war the Delaware Indians furnished 170 soldiers out of an adult male population of 218.

NOTE 9. Immediately after the close of the Revolutionary war, the United States Government made treaties with other tribes of Indians, and secured from them the very lands they had formerly acknowledged to belong to the Delawares, and the Delaware Indians received nothing whatever for the same. The tract consisted of several million acres, located in Ohio and Indiana.

NOTE 10. See Manypenny's report of how the Army Officers of Fort Leavenworth and other prominent persons assisted the settlers in making settlements on Delaware lands in Kansas, and by their actions finally discouraged the Delawares so much that they were forced in self-defense to sell their lands in Kansas and purchase homes in the Cherokee Nation, Indian Territory, a title to which was guaranteed by the United States Government. The same treaty also guaranteed them all civil rights and a voice in the Government of the Cherokee Nation. Now the Delaware Indians are forced to sue the Cherokees for this land at great expense to themselves, after they have paid for the lands and improvements more than $1,000,000.

Delaware Indian Pay House, 1868.

A

DELAWARE INDIAN

LEGEND

AND

THE STORY OF THEIR TROUBLES

BY

RICHARD C. ADAMS

REPRESENTING THE DELAWARE INDIANS

THE TREATY OF THE LENNI LENAPE OR DELAWARE INDIANS WITH WILLIAM PENN ON THE BANKS OF THE DELAWARE RIVER IN 1682.

WHEN the time arrived at which William Penn and the Indians had agreed to meet personally to confirm the treaty of peace and the purchase of the land which his commissioners had bargained for and the transaction was to be publicly ratified, Penn came accompanied by his friends of both sexes to the place where Philadelphia now stands. On his arrival he found the Chiefs and their people all assembled there. They were seen as far as the eye could reach, up the river, down the river and in the forest far beyond, and looked frightful, both on account of their numbers and their arms. The Quakers were but a handful in comparison with the Indians and were unarmed, but confidence in the justice of their cause prevented dismay and terror from seizing them. William Penn appeared in his usual clothes and was distinguished only by wearing a sky-blue sash of silk net-work around his waist. He had a roll of parchment containing a confirmation of the treaty of purchase and amity in his hands. One of the *Sachems*, who was the head Chief of them, put upon his own head a kind of chaplet in which appeared a small horn. This as among the primitive Nations and according to Scriptural language was an emblem of kingly power, and whenever the Chief who had the right to wear it put it on, it was understood that the place was made sacred and the persons of all present inviolable. Upon putting on this horn the Indians threw down their bows and arrows and seated themselves around the Chiefs in the form of a half moon upon the ground. The Chief Sachem then announced to William Penn, by means of an interpreter, that the Indians were ready to hear him. The treaty was ratified with all due solemnity and is known to this day as the treaty that never was sworn to and never was broken.

Chalkley, in his life of William Penn, says :

"It is much to be regretted when we have accounts of minor treaties between William Penn and the Indians, that in no history can be found an account of this, though so many make mention of it, and although all concur in considering it the most glorious in the annals of the world."

.

William Penn Treating With Delaware Indians, 1682.

THE STORY OF THEIR TROUBLES.

THE history of the Delaware Indians, perhaps, if given the attention of eminent writers, would be one of the most interesting, romantic, although pathetic stories, ever related by historians.

For more than three years I have been entrusted by my people with the responsibility of defending their rights and protecting their interests; and in discharging my trust as best I could or preparing myself for the duties required thereby, I have reviewed the history of many past events relating to them and their dealings, and not one have I ever found that was a discredit to them; neither have I found any cause to know why I, myself, should not be proud that I am a Delaware Indian.

Full justice has never been done the Indian in the American histories, and I should like to write one as it should be written from the Indian's own point of view. But while my whole heart and soul are devoted to them, I fear I could not do them credit in undertaking to relate their story; yet, some day, perhaps, I may try it.

In order that you may have a clear understanding of the condition of affairs, it will be necessary for me to give you, as briefly as possible, a history of the Delaware Indians from their first dealings with the white man down to the present time.

The Delaware Indians, or "Lenni Lenape," were once one of the most powerful tribes of Indians on the North American continent, the head of the Algonquins, called by many Indians "Our Grandfather." When first met by the white man they claimed and controlled all of the territory between the Hudson River and the Potomac.

Under the spreading elm tree at Shackamaxon, two hundred and seventeen years ago, they sold to the founder of the State of Pennsylvania, William Penn, the vast area within its borders for a nominal sum, and largely as an act of friendship and brotherly love which they entertained for the white people at that time and have ever since.

Sacred to the memory of the white man, as well as to that of the Delawares, has been the eventual treaty resulting from that transaction. In the rotunda of the Capitol at Washington may be seen the historical fresco recalling that event. But while the State of Pennsylvania has made rapid strides in progress, until now it ranks as one of the wealthiest and proudest States in the Union, the Delawares, who were so generous in years gone past, and who have always proved their loyalty to the United States Government, have been forced much against their will and their interest to cross the continent, unwilling but always yielding graciously, having utmost confidence in the promises that "this move will be the last," until now but a handful of them are left, where they have purchased homes in the Cherokee Nation, Indian Territory. And here, where they were assured by both the Cherokees and the United States Government that their rights and interests would be protected, they find that their very homes are now being covered with applications for mineral leases by both Cherokee citizens and citizens of the United States—wealthy corporations—who claim the protection of the United States Government and deny the rights of the Delaware Indians.

I appealed to the Indian Rights Association and others for their aid and moral support in defending our homes from the encroaching greed of grasping syndicates and companies who are now seeking to deprive us of one of the most sacred liberties mankind can claim—the right to control our own.

The Delaware Indians are more able to take care of their property, if given the opportunity of controlling it, than most of the white people who live in our country.

There are many things your civilized laws and public policy say are right that I cannot understand, but the greatest puzzle to me is,—Why is the Delawares' title to their lands now disputed and they required by the Government to appeal to the courts to obtain that which they bought and paid for with the advice, approval and guarantee of the United States Government itself? And even before that question is settled by the Courts, that they should be threatened with greater complications!

It may be because I am an Indian that I cannot understand the justice of this policy.

The good faith my people have shown: the prompt aid and assistance they have rendered the United States Government in the past as allies in the Revolutionary War; as soldiers and scouts in the Mexican and Civil wars; as guides for General Fremont across the Rocky Mountains; as peacemaker between other Indian tribes and the Federal Government, and the protection afforded by them to colonists in early days, of themselves are enough to entitle them to more land in bounties and grants, fifty times over, than the land now in question, which they bought and paid for.

The Cherokees now claim that the Delawares have no distinct rights in the Cherokee Nation. The Delawares claim the right to select one hundred and fifty-seven thousand six hundred acres of land for which they paid $157,600, and in addition to this an equal right with every native-born Cherokee in all the remaining lands and funds of the Cherokee Nation, for which they paid an additional sum of $121,824.28.

The history of this transaction is better understood by referring to the data that led up to it and the events that took place about that time, than by reading the contract or agreement itself.

You will see by referring to a letter on file in the Office of Indian Affairs, dated September 1st, 1866, and signed by D. N. Cooley, Commissioner of Indian Affairs, that the Delawares were offered lands in the Indian country, in the Seminole Nation at 15 cents per acre; in the Creek Nation at 30 cents per acre; or lands in the Quapaw Nation, the price to be determined when selections were made.

The Delawares were instructed, through their Agent, by letter dated October 13th, 1866, signed by John G. Pratt, to select a delegation and to " proceed South and select for your tribe a new reservation in that country." Accordingly the Delaware Council authorized Captain John Connor, head chief, Captain Sarcoxie, Charles Journeycake, Joseph Armstrong, Andrew Miller and Isaac Journeycake to proceed to the Indian country and select a new reservation.

On December 9th, 1866, the Delaware delegates, in company with the delegates on behalf of the Cherokee Nation, agreed upon and did select, " that part of the country on Little Verdigris or Caney, beginning at the Kansas line,

RESIDENCE OF CHARLES JOURNEYCAKE, CHIEF OF THE DELAWARES

where the 96th meridian crosses the same, and running thence east ten miles; thence south thirty miles; thence west ten miles; thence north to the place of beginning," the Delawares specifically declaring in the notice to the Cherokee Council that they preserve their tribal organization.

This selection was made in accordance with the instructions of the United States Government through the Commissioner of Indian Affairs, and the Delaware Indian Agent, and in accordance with the Act of the Delaware Council, and also the resolution of the Cherokee Council, of November 7th, 1866, which reads as follows:

" Resolved by the National Council, that the Principal Chief, Assistant Principal Chief, and three others, be appointed by the Principal Chief as Commissioners to enter into an agreement with the Delaware Delegation in reference to allowing the Delawares to select a reservation from our lands lying east or west of the 96th degree of longitude, according to the provisions of the treaty of July 19th, 1866.

| H. D. REESE, | JAMES VANN, |
| Clerk. | President National Council. |

Concurred,

| R. B. Ross, | JOHN YOUNG, |
| Clerk Council. | Speaker Council. |

Approved.

WM. P. Ross."

(See page 84, laws of the Cherokee Nation, 1839–1867.)

On April 8th, 1867, the Delaware-Cherokee Agreement was made and approved by the President of the United States, and in 1868, most of the Delawares moved to the Cherokee Nation and settled on the lands selected on Little Verdigris or Caney River, believing, as has been proved to my satisfaction by sworn statements of old Delawares, parties to the Agreement, and the Delaware Indian Agent, John G. Pratt, that this land was to be theirs and in no way was to be molested or interfered with by the Cherokee Indians; but after they had settled there, they were constantly annoyed by the Osages who also claimed the land, and a great many half-breed Cherokees, who would make raids amongst them. So, after being harassed on every side, they became greatly dissatisfied and all moved in a body to the Quapaw country, on Neosho River, expecting to get the Government to make an exchange of lands for them.

Superintendent Enoch Hoag and the Indian Agent finally persuaded them to return, telling them that they were not confined to the area of their previous selection, but were privileged to make their selection in any part of the Cherokee Nation where they could find good and suitable land.

Articles 4 and 5 of the Delaware treaty of July 4th, 1866, should also be taken into consideration, and also that part of Article 4 which says:

"The said tract of the country shall be set off with clearly and permanently marked boundaries by the United States, and also surveyed as Public lands are surveyed, *when the Delaware Council shall so request*, when the same may be in whole or in part allotted by said Council to each member of said tribe residing in said country."

Both the Delawares and Cherokees fully understood at the time of the Delaware-Cherokee Agreement, that the 157,600 acres of land was Delaware land, and in no part a portion of the Cherokee Nation or the Cherokee public domains. The Cherokee delegates, J. L. Adair and D. W. Bushyhead, in a communication addressed to the Senate Committee on Indian Affairs, on June 19th, 1890, said:

"As has been seen, the Delawares purchased one hundred and fifty-seven thousand six hundred acres of Cherokee lands, lying east of the 96th degree west longitude. That was an absolute and unconditional purchase, in which lands the Cherokee Nation has no title or interest."

(See Senate Bills 2322, 4005, 51st Congress.)

When the Delaware-Cherokee Agreement was made, the Delawares paid $157,600 for the right to select 157,600 acres of land.

They also bought for valuable consideration full citizenship in the Cherokee Nation, which would give them additional lands and an interest in their funds. A ratio was ascertained to determine what the Delawares should pay for this right, so a census of both tribes was taken; the assets of the Cherokees were fixed, and it was found that the ratio was one to thirteen and seventy-eight one-hundredths, and on this basis the Delawares paid an additional sum of $121,824.28.

The Cherokees claim the right, under the 15th article of the treaty of 1866, to sell to friendly Indians a separate and distinct tract of land east of the 96th meridian, or to sell to such Indians a communal or per capita interest in the lands and funds of the Cherokee Nation, or, in other words, a citizenship carrying with it all property rights. The Shawnees were admitted under the latter arrangement and for their citizenship paid $150,000. The Delawares sought to secure both rights (at the time having plenty of money), and the money was paid and received with such understanding.

In 1890 the Chief of the Cherokee Nation, J. B. Mayes, and the Cherokee delegates addressed a communication to the Committee on Indian Affairs, asking that the United States Government pay out per capita to the Delawares the trust funds, almost a million dollars, belonging to them, and giving as a reason for this request that the Delawares might be enabled to make permanent improvements upon their homes in the Cherokee Nation. This money was paid out to the Delawares per capita, and they have used the same to make good and substantial homes which are equal to any of those I have seen in the Eastern States. They have more than one hundred thousand acres of land in cultivation, although

numbering less than one thousand souls. Their land is under-
laid with valuable mineral deposits, such as lubricating oil,
gas, coal, etc. This seems to be their misfortune since they
are Indians. They have no money left in the hands of the
Government, and, if deprived of their rights in the Cherokee
Nation, they are paupers. If they win in their contention,
they are rich. The Cherokees are rich; they have a large
fund in the hands of the Government, made larger by
the money contributed to it by us. We have an interest in
this fund, but have no means of obtaining any portion of it
to defend our rights. So, thus disarmed, having by purchase
and improvements expended over one million dollars in lands
within the Cherokee Nation under the guaranteed protection
of the United States Government, as well as that of the Cherokees—are we thus to be left at their mercy?

Since the Delaware-Cherokee Agreement was made the
Cherokees have unlawfully admitted over 10,000 persons to
all the rights of citizenship and without compensation to the
Delawares, thereby reducing their interests in the communal
property, and disturbing the ratio on which the respective
rights of the Delawares and Cherokees were fixed. The
authorities of the Cherokee Nation, consisting principally of
the admitted class and intermarried white men, have done
everything they could to embarrass the Delawares.

They have questioned the rights of the Delawares in
sharing the communal property of the Cherokee Nation, and
even denied the rights of the heirs of the deceased Delawares
to the 157,600 acres of land that the Delawares purchased in
1867. This necessarily caused the Delawares to send representatives to Washington to protect their interests before the

A Group of Delaware Indians.

Congress of the United States and the Department of the Interior, or any other tribunal having authority in the premises.

Myself and John Bullette were appointed representatives and made Attorneys in Fact. Through our efforts the 25th section of the Curtis Bill became a law, which provides that suit may be brought in the Court of Claims and the Supreme Court to determine and enforce the rights of the Delawares in the lands and funds of the Cherokee Nation, and provides :

"That before any allotment shall be made of lands in the Cherokee Nation, there shall be segregated therefrom, by the Commission heretofore mentioned, in separate allotments or otherwise, the one hundred and fifty-seven thousand six hundred acres of land purchased by the Delaware tribe of Indians from the Cherokee Nation, under Agreement of April 8th, eighteen hundred and sixty-seven.

This, however, has not been done, although it has been demanded by us.

On August 4th, 1898, we brought suit in the Court of Claims, as provided by the Act of Congress referred to above, and have since been busily engaged in securing data, evidence and proofs necessary to sustain our contention.

They (the Cherokees) have not yet paid us the full amount of the money due us from the sale of the Outlet, which the highest courts of the land determined was ours (see Journey-cake Case, 28 C. Cls., R., 281 ; 155 U. S. R., 197), claiming that they did not have enough money to pay us in full. But they found enough money to appropriate nearly half a million dollars more than was required to pay the Freedmen of the Cherokee Nation, and in order that they might justify themselves in paying this money out, since they were to divide the greater part as attorney fees, the same authorities consented to and did place on the Freedmen roll more than one thousand negroes who, everyone knew, were not entitled to be placed on the roll.

A history of this shameful deal may be had by referring to Senate Document 101, 55th Congress, 3rd Session. This is a fair sample of the way the combination that has control of Cherokee affairs regards right and justice.

The same may be said in regard to the recent Agreement entered into with the Dawes Commission and the Commission on behalf of the Cherokee Nation, January 14th, 1899, in which it may be seen, by referring to section 6 of said Agreement, that the same authorities were willing to give to all the inter-married white persons and such other persons who were admitted without right or authority and without compensation to the Cherokee Nation, and even the negroes referred to above, an interest in all the lands and funds of the Cherokee Nation, equal to that due the legitimate owners, but expressly declared that nothing should be given to the Delawares, and section 87 of said Agreement seemed to annul the Curtis Act governing the segregation of the Delaware lands and even abrogating the entire Delaware-Cherokee Agreement itself. Said section 87 reads as follows:

" This agreement shall in nowise affect the provisions of existing treaties between the Cherokee Nation and the United States, except so far as it is inconsistent therewith, and no provisions of any Act of Congress now existing inconsistent with the Agreement shall be operative in the Cherokee Nation."

This Agreement, however, was not signed by the full-blood members of the Cherokee Nation, who have been our friends, neither was it ratified by Congress, and I have been

informed that the proposition was a surprise to the Dawes
Commission, but it was the best they could get. Hon. Henry
L. Dawes, in his letter transmitting the Agreement, said :

"The Commission are aware of many imperfections in this Agreement.
They have never been able to make one free from them."

And the Downing party of the Cherokee Nation, in order
to get the votes of that class of people whose rights to a division
in the lands and funds should be questioned, did endorse this
Agreement and made it a part of their platform, and by offering
an indirect bribe of an interest in the lands and funds for
votes did secure the election of their Chief and get control of
both branches of the Cherokee National Council, and will, of
course, attempt to further embarrass the Delaware Indians.

The same Act of Congress provides for the leasing of lands
in the Indian Territory, for the purpose of developing oil, coal,
asphalt and other minerals, leaving the matter optional and at
the discretion of the Secretary of the Interior to grant or reject
any or all applications that may be made for the same.

Before the Act of Congress referred to above certain
Cherokees and inter-married white men, relatives of the con-
stituted authorities of the Cherokee Nation, did secure what
they term mineral leases from the said authorities, covering
the homes and improvements of the Delaware Indians. They
did sub-lease the same to certain citizens of the United States
who claim to have expended twenty-odd thousand dollars in
putting down eighteen oil wells, and for this reason they
claimed a preferred right to lease from the Secretary of the
Interior over one hundred and eighty thousand acres of land,
covering most of the homes of the Delaware Indians, without
respect to their rights and without their consent.

One of the provisions of the leases is :

" Provided, That the domain or tract, or any part thereof above described, is not within or does not infringe upon the improvements or legal boundaries of any other citizen."

Notwithstanding the fact that we have invested over one million dollars in these identical lands and improvements thereon, these same people claimed in their petition to the Secretary of the Interior that there were no adverse claimants to this land ; and held that the expenditure of about twenty thousand dollars, if they were forced to lose it, would work a great hardship to them. They forget that they were trespassers on our land, and in justice should be compelled to pay us damages. They forget our rights and the hardship that might be imposed on us.

It might be noted, however, that no applications were filed for leases covering that portion of the Cherokee Nation where no Delawares were located.

The question as to the rights of the Delawares is now in the Court of Claims. If their contention is sustained that these lands are Delaware lands and not subject to the laws and constitution of the Cherokee Nation, the Cherokees have no right whatever to make these leases. But even if the Delaware lands were subject to the laws and constitution of the Cherokee Nation, there is a provision in the Delaware-Cherokee Agreement which says : " Nor shall the continued ownership and occupancy of said land by any Delaware so registered, be interfered with in any manner whatever without his consent," and the provision referred to above in the mineral lease would prevent them from interfering with the Delawares' rights.

The Delawares have just cause for alarm. If the pending leases are executed by the Secretary of the Interior, without

awaiting the decision of the Court of Claims as to the rights of the Delawares therein, that tribe will find its interests and remedies at law seriously embarrassed. The Supreme Court of the State of Oregon, in *Mosgrove vs. Harper*, May term, 1898, held that after the Secretary of the Interior had approved a lease of Indian lands he could not cancel the same, stating :

"That is a matter which belongs to the Judicial and not the Executive Department of the Government. The right of the lessee, when denied to re-enter and take possession of the leased premises under and by virtue of the several provisions of the lease, can only be tried out in a court of law, and not by some Executive Department of the Government."

The Assistant Attorney-General for the Interior Department, in his opinion dated June 12th, 1899, regarding certain leases covering Ponca Indian lands, Oklahoma Territory, in which it was shown that fraud existed in the procurement of the same, and upon which payment of royalties have since been accepted by the Interior Department, says :

" It is impossible to avoid the conclusion that with full knowledge of the fraud practised in their procurement, these leases have been affirmed and the lessee permitted to proceed on that theory to such an extent that to cancel or rescind the leases at this time because of that fraud would not comport with the principles of reciprocal justice."

In one of my protests to the Secretary, I said :

" The various companies have employed prominent attorneys and many of the parties interested hold high and honorable positions both in political and social circles. Their cause has been well represented and they are in position to represent it well, while I, the representative of the Delaware Indians, have none of these advantages ; yet I feel that I have the best right to claim your attention and your careful consideration of the truth of the allegations I have set forth. In conclusion, I would ask that all leases be declared void and that no leases be granted in the Cherokee Nation, at least until the Delaware lands have been segregated by the Dawes Commission as instructed by the 25th Section of the Act of Congress, known as the Curtis Bill."

On July 17th, 1899, Hon. Thomas Ryan, Acting Secretary of the Interior, in his letter of instructions to the United States

Indian Inspector for the Indian Territory, rejected the applications of the various companies who made applications for the leases covering the lands of the Delaware Indians, but leaves the impression that they may still obtain leases if they could prove that there were no adverse claimants to the land and made applications as prescribed by the instructions of the Secretary of the Interior, May 22nd, 1899.

A great many prominent and influential gentlemen, whose attention was called to the condition of affairs which confronted the Delawares, kindly responded and protested in our behalf. Among them were Hon. R. F. Pettigrew. Chairman of the Committee on Indian Affairs in the Senate : Hon. James S. Sherman, Chairman of the Committee on Indian Affairs in the House of Representatives ; Hon. Charles Curtis, Member of the Committee on Indian Affairs of the House of Representatives ; Hon. Matthew S. Quay, United States Senator ; Rev. T. J. Morgan, Ex-Commissioner of Indian Affairs : Hon. Darwin R. James, Chairman of the Board of Indian Commissioners ; S. M. Brosius, Esq., Agent of the Indian Rights Association, Washington, D. C., and a great many others.

We are now trying to secure our last little homes in the Indian Territory and protect them from the grasping greed of heartless syndicates and corporations. We have defended our interests as best we could ; we greatly need the assistance of the Christian influence of this great Nation, and we shall be grateful for the help that we believe you will render us.

With every sentiment of respect, I am your obedient servant,

RICHARD C. ADAMS,

Representing the Delaware Indians.

DELAWARE BAPTIST CHURCH.

LETTERS AND AGREEMENT.

THE following are copies of some letters written by officials of the Government, which may be found on file in the Office of the Commissioner of Indian Affairs, Washington, D. C. They will assist the reader in forming some idea of the manner in which the Delawares have been dealt with :

Piqua, *Mar. 20, 1821.*

Sir :

On the 15th inst., I received from his Excellency, Gov. Cass, a letter of which an extract will be found above.

The Delaware Nation as joint owners with the Miamies occupied the country watered by the White River in the State of Indiana. It might be estimated safely at the time of the treaty of St. Mary's of Oct., 1818, in extent at 100 miles by 70. There is no tract of the same magnitude to which the Indian title has been extinguished within the last 20 years of greater value, the soil is good, is well watered and the climate fine. The permanent seat of Government for the State of Indiana has been lately fixed in the centre of the White River tract. This country must greatly enrich the public treasury. It was with the utmost difficulty that the Delawares could be induced to relinquish their claim for it. They were pressed repeatedly and for years on the subject. The negotiations were finally undertaken at the earnest solicitations of the Governor and Legislature of Indiana, expressed to the President, and never was any undertaking of the kind more difficult to accomplish. The joint ownership of the Miamies greatly added to our embarrassments on the occasion, in proportion to the difficulties that presented themselves so were we liable in our promises. The communications made by myself to your excellency by the Chief Anderson, would convey some idea of what the Delawares had a right to expect. They have reason to expect that a country should be immediately provided for them west of the Mississippi and that they were to be protected in the peaceable enjoyment of that country. This country was to be designated by a certain prominent geographical boundary, It was not understood how large it should be but as the chief design of their removal was to live as hunters, and to get out of the immediate neighbourhood of the whites, they had a right to expect a country sufficiently large for the purposes of hunting. I would suppose in any event it would not be less than the one which they left. It was not apprehended that land far interior with you was of much consequence and the understanding with the Delaware Chiefs was that their

41

station should be as remote as their safety from the other tribes would allow. Previous to their removal last year, the contents of a letter from the Secretary of War, Jan. 6, 1820, together with a copy of yours to him of the preceding November, was communicated to the Chiefs (copies are enclosed). I recommended also, to them to prefer the hilly country on account that they would not so soon be interrupted by the approaches of the whites; I recommended also, that they should select their future home as far from the whites as their own safety would permit.

The Delawares were promised reasonable supplies of corn, salt and ammunition for the first year after their arrival in your country. The one-half of the tribe yet remain here and will move some time in the coming summer. This Nation was always a leading one among the Indians of this country. They are significantly distinguished on all public occasions as Grand Fathers. Should their settlement with you be in all respects agreeable to their feelings, it may have a decided influence in drawing all our Indians westward. It is now equally their interest as well as ours that they should leave this country. There is no tribe of the natives on this continent whose case affords so many causes to excite the best sympathies of our nature.

They are the descendants of the primitive inhabitants of the lower counties of Pennsylvania, of the State of Delaware and the adjacent parts of New Jersey. There are persons of this tribe with you, and they are not a few, that were born and raised within sixty miles of Philadelphia. In contending with the whites for what they considered their just rights, they have been reduced to a mere handful. Every consideration of justice, of humanity and sound policy requires that they should be treated with liberality.

My feelings as an individual are largely interested for them, having been their Agent for a considerable part of my life, there is not an individual that is not personally known to me. I pray your Excellency to have special care taken of them, to supply their immediate and most pressing wants and to have them permanently fixed agreeably to their wishes.

The number of Delawares yet to go from this country is not much short of one thousand souls. You may expect them in the course of this year.

> I have the honor to remain,
> With great respect,
> Your obt. servant,
> JOHN JOHNSTON.

His Excellency,
William Clark,
St. Louis.

NOTE: While it is evident from this letter that the Delawares surrendered in Indiana 4,480,000 acres of land, they received as a reservation less than 1,000,000 acres of land in Kansas, and as an Outlet estimated at one million acres. This

43

outlet, however, brought the Delaware Indians only $10,000, which was paid to five chiefs for certain reasons and the Delaware people received no part of it.

UPPER PIQUA,
October 22, 1821.

Sir:

I have now to acknowledge the receipt of your letter of the 23rd August, covering an extract from Mr. Graham's letter to you of the 27th July last. I had at different periods communicated to Governor Cass all the information that was necessary in relation to the Delawares. It is presumed that Mr. Graham has not had a view of any of my communications. Until recently I was of the opinion that Governor Clark still had the superintendence of Indian Affairs west of the Mississippi.

A personal annuity for life was solemnly guaranteed by the Commissioner of the United States and myself at the Treaty of St. Mary's to Anderson and Lapanihlie, the two principal chiefs of the Delaware Nation, that is to say $360 to the former and $140 to the latter. On this part of the negotiation the personal safety of the Chiefs required the utmost secrecy. I presume there is no record of the stipulation on the journals of the Commissioners. The Government is pledged for the regular payment of these two annuities ; each of the Chiefs hold a paper written and signed by myself to this purport. Anderson is now about sixty years old and Lapanihlie fifty. The great difficulties which occurred in purchasing the country of the Delawares made us liberal in promises.

The Government and citizens of Indiana took such a deep interest in the event that a purchase must have been made. It fell to my lot to arrange all the details of the treaty with the Delawares. I have since had reason to regret that many of my engagements were not written more in detail in that instrument. My embarrassments in moving those people for the want of funds has been extremely great. I am now in debt as the Agent of the Government to sundry individuals on account of sundry claims which the Nation had against us, to the amount of $2,415.67.

I intended to have submitted this business to you through Governor Cass sometime before the meeting of Congress, to the end that provision might be made to relieve me, but as your letter has brought the case of the Delawares into view, I submit it now with a request that if it is within the means of the Department I may be furnished with money to pay it. I have regular vouchers for the whole amount.

By the treaty of Fort Wayne of 1803, the Delawares and other tribes who were parties to it, were to receive annually forever one hundred and fifty bushels of salt. In apportioning this quantity among the whole, I assigned to the Delawares thirty bushels yearly. 30 bushels of salt and the transportation would amount at that time to $100. The salt was not furnished regularly until it was quite evident it never would be furnished regularly and as the Nation were leaving me forever, I thought it best to allow them money in lieu of it. This would put an end to all difficulties thereafter and would not prejudice the Government. I respectfully recommend that the arrangement made with the Chiefs be approved.

There is nothing due the Delawares for arrears of salt. The articles which I furnished them previous to their departure was in full discharge of all claims prior to their leaving us. They have lost horses on their journey westward, which they claim compensation for, and which if stolen by the whites they should be paid for.

The following is a list of debts due on account of moving the Delawares in 1820 and 1821. The amount has no connection with the current expenses of my agency.

To the house of Neave & Brother, of Cincinnati, for powder, lead, tobacco and flints $532.68
To Connor & Marshall of Indiana, for provisions and ammunition and for extra services for interpreting . . . . 993.
To Neave & Bro. of Cincinnati for sundry articles of merchandize to make satisfaction for a murder committed on a Delaware Indian by a citizen of the U. S. $151.10
To Benjamin Brandon of Piqua, Ohio, for flour, beef and salt . . $523.75
For carriage of goods from Cincinnati to Wapaghkonetta 48.43
To Benjamin S. Cox, of Piqua, Ohio, for 4 saddles and 4 saddles . $76.00
To William Johnston, of Piqua, Ohio, for sundry articles of merchandize $94.65
To Nicholas Greenham of Piqua for sundry articles of merchandize $53.95
To Francis Duchoquet, expenses to White river express $6.00
To ——— Snively for 1 rifle to the Chief, the Buck $20.00
To John Johnston for flour and meat $114.20

$2,415.67

On account of the number of poor Delawares who last moved, I was under the necessity of procuring for them forty horses at thirty dollars each. A paper enclosed will more fully explain the transaction.

The $1,200 is to be remitted here in the spring and deducted from the annuity of 1822. I have only further to remark in relation to the Delawares that sound policy as well as humanity requires that they should be treated with the utmost liberality in the country to which they have gone, if their new situation should prove agreeable to them, they will be the means of drawing all the Indians in this country after them. It is now unquestionably the interest of all to move, for they cannot be civilized on what is called Reservations, that is small portions of land surrounded by a numerous white population.

I am informed that measures will be taken to induce the Government to organize a principal and independent agency at Sandusky for the

Wyandottes. Such a measure would be totally unnecessary. The small number of Indians in that quarter (and they are constantly diminishing) does not require any such establishment. Mr. Shaw as Sub-Agent at Upper Sandusky for the Wyandottes and Mr. Montgomery sub-agent for the Senecas below. The Department as at present organized is fully adequate to all the reasonable and just wants of the Indians. At the payment of the annuities in July last, at Upper Sandusky, I received the thanks of the Chiefs of both Nations for the satisfactory manner in which their business was conducted. I should be ashamed to have less to do than at present.

I know not whether I am entitled to receive the laws of the United States. I have formerly applied for them at the War Department, as well as the Department of State. They were not sent. In discharging the duties of my office, I am frequently in great need of the laws. The volume which contains the substance of all the statutes having reference to the public lands would assist me much in my official duties.

I have the honor to remain,
With great respect,
Sir, your obt. servant,

The Honorable J. C. Calhoun,
JOHN JOHNSTON,
Secretary of War,
Indian Agent.
Washington.

(Delaware C, 1486.)

DELAWARE AGENCY,
June 16, 1855.

Sir :

Since the ejection of intruders from the Delaware Trust lands by military force, is no longer to be looked for; by request of the Chiefs and principal men of that tribe, I would most respectfully call the attention of the Department at Washington to the importance of a separate survey and sale of the lands. The late act of Congress of the 3rd of March intended to enable the President to carry out in good faith the recent treaties of the Ottoes, Missouris, etc. Instead of checking intrusion on these " trust lands," as was confidently expected, seems to be regarded by many as a license to enter upon them. The slip from a Kansas paper, herewith enclosed, exhibits the extraordinary and unprincipled spirit actuating the unprincipled portion of the squatter emigration. The difficulty of a faithful execution of the treaty will but increase with time. A long, uninterrupted possession gives even the trespasser a color of right, and quiet peaceable citizens are inclined to respect such rights. A large emigration is daily flowing into the country, seizing upon the best lands and most desirable situations, uniting with and giving strength and power to unlawful combinations. In a word, should the sale be long delayed, I do not believe these lands will bring at auction one-half of their value. I have thus briefly called up this unpleasant subject, from a sincere desire that justice may be done those of all others the most helpless and inoffensive people.

Very respectfully,

Your obt. servant,

B. F. Robinson,

Indian Agent.

Col. A. Cumming,

Supt. Indian Affairs.

Enclosure.

Squatters' Meeting.

At a meeting of the squatters, on Saturday, March 10, in Leavenworth, after much discussion upon two reports of a committee, the following was adopted.

Whereas, It has now become apparent that pre-emption will be assured to the settlers upon the land ceded to the U. S. by the Delaware Indians, therefore be it—

1. Resolved, That on and after the first day of May next, we will take the pre-emption law as our sole guide and rule of action in relation to claims in the Delaware District and our Squatter Courts are hereby instructed to act accordingly.

2. That where the existing laws and regulations of this Association shall clash or differ with the Pre-emption Law, they are so far declared to be void and of no effect.

3. That we tender our grateful acknowledgement to Hon. J. Whitfield and other distinguished friends, both in and out of Congress, for their able and indefatigable exertions in our behalf, which has greatly strengthened our cause and shown our just claims for consideration at the hands of the Government.

4. That the proceedings of this meeting be published in the Kansas Herald, Squatters' Sovereign, and Kansas Pioneer, and such Missouri journals as feel friendly to the squatters' cause.

R. R. Reese, Chairman.

(Delaware T, 413.)

Elwood, Kan., March 22, 1862.

Hon. Lyman Trumbull,

Dear Sir :

I wish some information about the Delaware Indians. I will just state that our Senators, Lane and Pomeroy, in speeches and otherwise, urged the settlement of those lands and as a consequence about 2,000 people are upon those lands, many of them refugees from oppression in Missouri, desiring to make homes for their families in the truly loyal State of Kansas.

Now we have recently heard that they will be driven from there to make room for an imaginary railroad company, who, I believe, will not come up to their agreement with the Government.

They have advertised to sell said lands and take one-third of the purchase money, when if a man comes with five dollars, they will take it and make out his papers for $50, $100, or $200, and get all they can.

They also have Agents in all the towns around to sell land and if they cannot sell lands, sell the timber off the lands for firewood, rail and saw timber, at a small price. I will send you one of their notices. The timber is being cut at a dreadful rate now.

Sir, if they had the lands "bona fide," would they thus wilfully destroy the timber? I have recently passed through the reserve and the timber near Lawrence and Oskaloosa is very much destroyed already,

I hope, sir, you will call the attention of the President to these facts and let me know all about it by letter.

I dislike troubling our Senators at this time, but it is an important matter to at least 2,000 as good and loyal people as there are to be found.

And endorsing your course as a statesman for many years, I have taken the liberty to time your time and patience.

Please write at your earliest convenience and give me all the information you can.

Please send us occasionally some public documents.

Very respectfully,
Your friend,
P. C. FERGUSON.

Hon. W. P. DOLE,
Commissioner Indian Affairs,
DEAR SIR:
Allow me to call your attention to within.

L. TRUMBULL.

(Book No. 70, page 516.)

DEPARTMENT OF THE INTERIOR,
OFFICE OF INDIAN AFFAIRS,
WASHINGTON, D. C., May 29, 1863.

F. JOHNSON, Esq,
U. S. Agent,
Quindaro, Kansas.
SIR:

Your letter of the 24th ultimo, enclosing the request of the Delaware Chiefs for permission to apply $800 of their funds to the purpose of defraying the expenses of a delegation to the Rocky Mountains to select a new location for the Delaware Nation, has been received. Official information received here from every portion of the country mentioned, fully satisfies me that there is no locality in all that region that is not subject to very grave objections, for the contemplated purpose. Throughout the whole of Utah, the lands with scarcely any exception can only be cultivated by irrigation and a very large portion are simply barren waste. To the North and Northeast the country is wild, rocky and mountainous, inhabited mainly by wild tribes of Indians, with whom no treaties for the extinguishment of titles have been negotiated and who are much addicted to hostilities as well amongst themselves as towards white emigration passing through the country. I feel well assured that a movement of the Delawares to any portion of that country could not result advantageously and would probably prove disastrous. For these reasons, I feel constrained to withhold my assent to the request of the Chiefs. I am *not adverse, but on the contrary greatly desire a removal of the Delawares* from Kansas, provided they can find a location in the Indian country that can be obtained as a permanent home. All the acccounts concur in representing this country as one of the most desirable in all our borders and the best suited to the peculiar wants of the Indians. Its climate is delightful, its soil is fertile and its geographical position is such that its occupation by lawless whites can be more easily prevented than any other portion of the country with which I am acquainted. By common consent this country seems to be recognized as the Indian country and I have strong hopes that it will eventually prove for them a happy and prosperous home. To render it so, no effort on my part will be wanting. You are directed to submit this letter to the Chiefs and should they so desire, are authorized to grant them permission to appropriate so much of their funds as is in your judgment actually necessary to defray the expenses of a delegation to the Indian country for the purpose of examining the same and ascertaining what arrangements can be made with a view to securing a permanent home for those of the Delawares who may desire to emigrate.

Very respectfully,
Your obedient servant,
WILLIAM P. DOLE,
Commissioner.

DELAWARE INDIAN DELEGATES TO WASHINGTON, 1866, AND PARTIES TO
DELAWARE-CHEROKEE AGREEMENT, 1867.

DELAWARE-CHEROKEE AGREEMENT.

ARTICLES OF AGREEMENT

MADE this 8th day of April, A. D. 1867, between the Cherokee Nation, represented by William P. Ross, Principal Chief, Riley Keys, and Jesse Bushyhead, delegates, duly authorized, parties of the first part, and the Delaware tribe of Indians, represented by John Connor, Principal Chief, Charles Journeycake, Assistant Chief, Isaac Journeycake, and John Sarcoxie, delegates for and on behalf of said Delaware tribe, duly authorized, witnesseth :

Whereas, By the 15th article of a certain treaty between the United States and the Cherokee Nation ratified August 11th, 1866, certain terms were provided, under which friendly Indians might be settled upon unoccupied lands in the Cherokee county, east of the line of 96th degree of west longitude, the price to be paid for such lands to be agreed on by the Indians to be thus located and the Cherokee Nation, subject to the approval of the President of the United States ; and whereas, by a treaty between the United States and the Delaware tribe of Indians ratified August 10th, 1866, the removal of the said Delawares to the Indian country south of Kansas was provided for, and in the 4th article whereof an agreement was made by the United States to sell to the Delawares a tract of land, being part of a tract a cession of which by the Cherokees to the United States was then contemplated ; and whereas, no such cession of land was made by the Cherokees to the United States, but in lieu thereof, terms were provided as hereinbefore mentioned, under which friendly Indians might be settled upon their lands ; and whereas, a full and free conference has been held between the representatives of the Cherokees and the Delawares, in view of the treaties herein referred to, *first looking to a location of the Delawares upon the Cherokee lands, second and their consolidation with said Cherokee Nation :* Now therefore, it is agreed between the parties hereto, subject to the approval of the President of the United States, as follows ;

The Cherokees, parties of the first part, for and in consideration of certain payments and the fulfillment of certain conditions, hereinafter mentioned, agree to sell to the Delawares, a quantity of land east of the line of the 96th degree west longitude, in the aggregate equal to 160 acres of land for each individual of the Delaware tribe who has been enrolled upon a certain register made February 18th, 1867, by the Delaware Agent, and on file in the Office of Indian Affairs, being the list of the Delawares who elect to remove to the " Indian country " to which list may be added, only with the consent of the Delaware Council the names of such other Delawares as may within one month after the signing of this agreement, desire to be added thereto ; and the selection of the lands to be purchased by the Delawares may be made by said Delawares in any part of the Cherokee reservation east of said line of 96 degrees, not already selected and in possession of other parties ; and in case the Cherokee lands shall hereafter be allotted among the members of said Nation, it is agreed that the aggregate amount of land herein provided for the Delawares, to include their improvements according to the legal sub-divisions, when surveys are made (that is to say, 160 acres for each individual), shall be guaranteed to each Delaware incorporated by these articles into the Cherokee Nation ; nor shall the continued ownership and occupancy of said land by any Delaware so registered be interfered with in any manner whatever without his consent, but shall be subject to the same conditions and restrictions as are by the laws of the Cherokee Nation imposed upon the native citizens thereof: Provided That nothing herein shall confer the right to alienate, convey or dispose of any such lands, except in accordance with the constitution and laws of said Cherokee Nation.

And the said Delawares, parties of the second part, agree that there shall be paid to the said Cherokees, from the Delaware funds now held or hereafter received by the United States, a sum of money equal to one dollar per acre, for the whole amount of 160 acres of land, for every individual Delaware who has already been registered upon the aforesaid list, made February 18th, 1867, with the additions thereto heretofore provided for. And the Secretary of the Interior is authorized and requested to sell any United States stocks belonging to the Delawares, to procure funds necessary to pay for said lands; but in case he shall not feel authorized, under existing treaties, to sell such bonds belonging to the Delawares, it is agreed that he may transfer such U. S. bonds to the Cherokee Nation, at their market value at the date of such transfer. And the said Delawares further agree that there shall be paid from their funds, now or hereafter to come into possession of the United States, a sum of money which shall sustain the same proportion to the existing Cherokee National Fund that the number of Delawares registered as above mentioned, and removing to the Indian country, sustains to the whole number of Cherokees residing in the Cherokee Nation; and for the purpose of ascertaining such relative numbers, the registers of the Delawares herein referred to, with such additions as may be made within one month from the signing of this agreement, shall be the basis of calculation as to the Delawares, and an accurate Census of the Cherokees residing in the Cherokee Nation shall be taken under the laws of the Nation within four months, and properly certified copies thereof filed in the Office of Indian Affairs, which shall be the basis of calculation as to the Cherokees. And that there may be no doubt hereafter as to the amount to be contributed to the Cherokee National Fund by the Delawares, it is hereby agreed by the parties hereto that the whole amount of the invested funds of the Cherokees, after deducting all just claims thereon, is $678,000. And the Delawares further agree that in calculating the total amount of said National Fund there shall be added to the said sum of $678,000 the sum of $1,000,000, being the estimated value of the Cherokee neutral lands in Kansas, thus making the whole Cherokee National Fund $1,678,000; and this last mentioned sum shall be taken as the basis for calculating the amount which the Delawares are to pay into the common fund : Provided, That as the $678,-000 of funds now on hand belonging to the Cherokees is chiefly composed of stocks of different values, the Secretary of the Interior may transfer from the Delawares to the Cherokees a proper proportion of the stocks now owned by the Delawares, of like grade and value, which transfer shall be in part of the pro rata contribution herein provided for by the Delawares to the funds of the Cherokee Nation ; but the balance of the pro rata contribution by the Delawares to said funds shall be in cash or U. S. bonds at their market value. All cash and all proceeds of stocks, whenever the same may fall

due or be sold, received by the Cherokees from the Delawares
under this agreement, shall be invested and applied in accordance with the 23rd article of the treaty with the Cherokees
of August 11th, 1866.

On the fulfillment by the Delawares of the foregoing stipu-
lations, all the members of the tribe registered as above provided shall become members of the Cherokee Nation, with the
same rights and immunities and the same participation (and
no other) in the National Funds as Native Cherokees, save as
hereinbefore provided.

And the children hereafter born of such Delawares so
incorporated into the Cherokee Nation, shall in all respects be
regarded as Native Cherokees.

WM. P. ROSS, Principal Chief:

RILEY KEYS,
Cherokee Delegation.

JOHN X CONNER, Principal Chief;
his
mark

CHARLES JOURNEYCAKE,

ISAAC JOURNEYCAKE,

JOHN X SARCOXIE,
his
mark
Delaware Delegation.

Executed and delivered in our presence by the above
named delegates of the Cherokee and Delaware Nations, at
the city of Washington, in the district of Columbia, the day
and year first above written.

JOHN G. PRATT.

WM. A. PHILLIPS.

EDWARD S. MENAGER.

DEPARTMENT OF THE INTERIOR,
April 11, 1867.

The within agreement between the Cherokee and Delaware tribes of Indians, concluded on the 8th inst., and providing for uniting the two tribes as contemplated by the Cherokee treaty of July 19, 1866, is respectfully submitted to the President, with the recommendation that it be approved.

O. H. BROWNING,
Secretary.

Approved April 11, 1867.

ANDREW JOHNSON.

Ratified by the National Committee, June 15, 1867.

H. D. REESE,	SMITH CHRISTIE,
Clerk Nat. Committee.	*President Nat. Committee.*

Concurred in.

S. FOREMAN,	JOHN YOUNG,
Clerk of Council.	*Speaker of Council.*

———

RESOLUTION IN FURTHERANCE OF THE TREATY WITH THE DELAWARES.

Resolved, by the National Council, That the Principal Chief be and he is hereby authorized to appoint some suitable person to transcribe the Cherokee Census rolls, and forward copies of them to the Secretary of the Interior at as early a date as it can be done. Also, to call on the Secretary of the Interior for a copy of the Delaware census roll.

Tahlequah, C. N., June 17, 1867.

Approved.

WM. P. ROSS,
Principal Chief.

(The italicized lines and notes are placed in the above copy to call the attention of the reader to particular features of the Agreement; they are not found in the original. Perhaps if this Agreement had been drawn up by lawyers of the present day, it would not have been such an ambiguous document.)

RESIDENCE OF JOHN YOUNG, A DELAWARE INDIAN.

REPORT OF THE COMMISSIONER OF INDIAN AFFAIRS, 1869.

Pages 484 and 485.

"THE sale of bonds, indicated in the preceding table, which were previously held in trust, for the Delaware general fund, was effected by a transfer upon the trust-fund books of the Department on the 13th of May, 1869, to the credit of the Cherokee funds, in accordance with the wishes of the Delaware Indians, an agreement having been previously made (April 8, 1867) between the Cherokee and Delaware Indians, based upon prior treaties, by which the Cherokees agreed to sell to the said Delaware Indians a portion of their land east of a line of ninety-six degrees of west longitude at the rate of one dollar per acre, upon condition that the said Delaware Indians, in addition to the amount necessary to pay for said land, transfer to the credit of the different Cherokee funds a pro rata share of their trust funds, and become a part of the Cherokee Nation.

It was found by calculation that 985 Delaware Indians would require, at 160 acres each, 157,600 acres, amounting at one dollar per acre to.............................. $157,600.00

The proportion of the number of Delawares to that of the Cherokees was found to be as 1 to 13.78, and on this basis the amount of stocks which it was found necessary to transfer to the Cherokees, as pro rata funds from those belonging to the Delawares, was.......................... 121,824.28

Total amount acquired to cover payment for 157,600 acres of land and pro rata funds transferred $279,424.28

60

The funds transferred were as follows:
Amount of non-paying bonds of
several Southern States as shown in
the above statement, transferred at
par, as per agreement................... $32,000.00
Amount of paying stocks of State
of Missouri............................. 2,000.00

$34,000.00

$230,716.10 in United States bonds issued to
Union Pacific Railway Company, eastern divi-
sion, transferred at market rates (106¾.)......... 245,424.28

$279,424.28 "

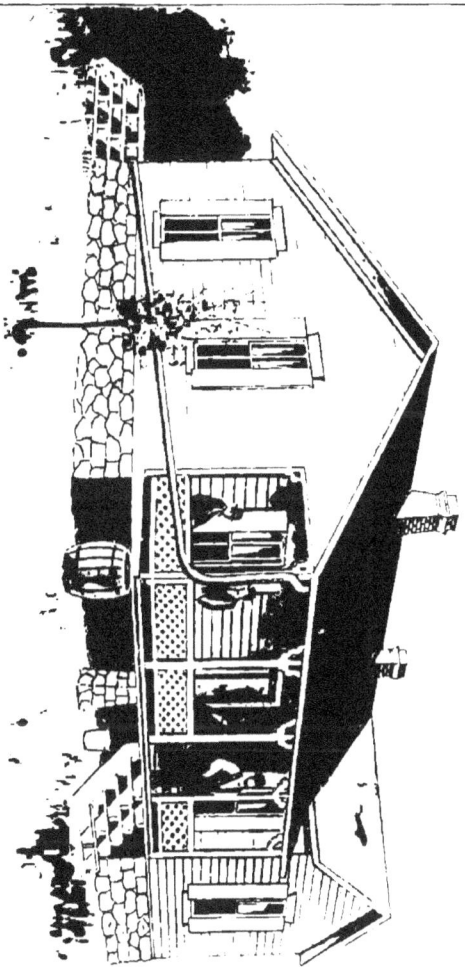

RESIDENCE OF JOB PARKER

CONCLUSION.

IF the kind reader into whose hands this booklet may chance to fall should become sufficiently interested in the matters relating to the Delaware Indians to render them moral support and assistance in any manner, such assistance will be greatly appreciated by both the Delaware people and your humble servant.

In distributing, with my compliments, a limited number of these booklets, I have undertaken the task from my own personal resources, and owing to my want of funds have not been able to make the distribution very large : but should you, or your friends, wish other copies of it, upon receipt of a remittance I will cheerfully furnish them.

The Delaware Indians, having no fund at their disposal, have been able to promise me so far only a contingent fee, and for three years, at my own personal expense, I have championed their cause and the cost of doing this has been many thousand dollars.

While I have undertaken to attend to matters personally before the Executive Departments of the Government, it is very necessary to have able attorneys represent us before the Judiciary and this has been one of the great expenses of this cause.

We were fortunate, however, in securing as attorney of record before the Court of Claims the assistance of Hon. Walter S. Logan, President of the New York State Bar Association, and as Associate Counsel, Marx E. Harby, of the firm of Logan, Demond & Harby, No. 27 William Street, New York.

The purpose of distributing these booklets is to better inform the public as to the justice of our cause. Few men will do another knowingly a willful wrong and there are but few men who will not be good Samaritans if they but have the opportunity.

With every sentiment of respect,

I am, sincerely yours,

RICHARD C. ADAMS,

Representing the Delaware Indians,

Washington, D. C.

ADDENDA.

AND now you've read their story and their Legend, too,
  You see by these traditions that they were friends to you.
You see the needs and troubles of this persecuted band,
Who always have stood by you, and helped you to a man.
Greater proof of friendship than this could never be,
When the quarrel was not his, he gave his blood for thee!
And now he asks your friendship, but not at such a cost,
He's asking your assistance, before his home is lost.

He fears not the judgment when he gets to Court,
His rights are firmly anchored as any ship in port,
But there are pirates in the Harbor!   Fierce marauders lurking near !
And the mischief they are planning is the danger he may fear.
They are seeking to deprive us of the product of our land.
They care not who may own it, if they but perfect their plan.
In this bloodless battle, can we now expect your aid ?
Give us for the blood we've spilt, your moral help instead.

R. C. A.

WALTER S. LOGAN,
Attorney of Record for Delaware Indians.

MARX E. HARBY,
Associate Counsel.

THE LEGEND OF THE "YÁH QÚA WHÉE" OR MASTODON.

LONG AGO, in time almost forgotten, when the Indians and the Great Spirit knew each other better, when the Great Spirit would appear and talk with the wise men of the Nation, and they would counsel with the people; when every warrior understood the art of nature, and the Great Spirit was pleased with his children; long before the white man came and the Indians turned their ear to the white man's God; when every warrior believed that bravery, truth, honesty and charity were the virtues necessary to take him to the happy hunting-grounds; when the Indians were obedient and the Great Spirit was interested in their welfare, there were mighty beasts that roamed the forests and plains.

The Yáh Qúa Whée or mastodon that was placed here for the benefit of the Indians was intended as a beast of burden, and to make itself generally useful to the Indians. This beast rebelled. It was fierce, powerful and invincible, its skin being so strong and hard that the sharpest spears and arrows could scarcely penetrate it. It made war against all other animals that dwelt in the woods and on the plains which the Great Spirit had created to be used as meat for his children—the Indians.

A final battle was fought and all the beasts of the plains and forests arrayed themselves against the mastodon. The Indians were also to take part in this decisive battle if necessary, as the Great Spirit had told them they must annihilate the mastodon.

71

The great bear was there and was wounded in the battle.

The battle took place in the Ohio Valley, west of the Alleghanies. The Great Spirit descended and sat on a rock on the top of the Alleghanies to watch the tide of battle. Great numbers of the mastodons came, and still greater numbers of the other animals.

The slaughter was terrific. The mastodons were being victorious until at last the valleys ran in blood. The battle field became a great mire, and many of the mastodons, by their weight, sank in the mire and were drowned.

The Great Spirit became angry at the mastodon, and from the top of the mountain hurled bolts of lightning at their sides until he killed them all except one large bull, who cast aside the bolts of lightning with his tusks and defied everything, killing many of the other animals in his rage, until at last he was wounded. Then he bounded across the Ohio river, over the Mississippi, swam the Great Lakes, and went to the far north where he lives to this day.

Traces of that battle may yet be seen. The marshes and mires are still there, and in them the bones of the mastodon still are found as well as the bones of many other animals.

There was a terrible loss of the animals that were made for food for the Indians, in that battle, and the Indians grieved much to see it, so the Great Spirit caused, in remembrance of that day, the cranberry to come and grow in the marshes to be used as food, its coat always bathed in blood, in remembrance of that awful battle.

NOTE. The foregoing is one of the many Delaware Indian legends. I have never seen it in print, and thinking it may be of some interest to the mythological student, I relate it here. R. C. A.

TO THE DELAWARE INDIANS.

I HAVE travelled o'er the country that once was our domain,
Seen the rivers and the mountains, the broad and fertile plain,
Where the Indian chased the buffalo, the antelope and deer,
When the smoke from Indian wigwams arose from far and near ;
Seen the lovely Susquehanna, where our council fire would burn,
And all the tribes and warriors would gather there to learn
The wise teachings of our chieftains and their traditions old,
And to tell it to their children as to them it had been told.

I see, from time immemorial, by stories handed down,
We had exclusive title to our homes and hunting-ground,
But then there came some pilgrims from a far and distant shore,
As they said " with Christian motives," our country to explore ;
For us, " a poor heathen nation," their hearts were truly sad ;
And to save us from " the infernal powers " they'd be very glad.
But to provide the daily bread of those who laid the plan,
Well, of course, we'd be expected to give them plenty of land.

But for that we should not care, they would lead us on to light,
And " in heaven we'll be rewarded " they say, for doing right,
For there the Bible teaches, " our treasures we should store ; "
" If our rights are there established, we need for nothing more."
" And Christians will gladly show us the path the pilgrims trod,
That leads unto eternal joy in paradise with God."
So we gave close attention to their actions one by one,
And this, as we have found it, is part that they have done.

They took with pious gratitude the land that was our own,
They killed the buffalo and deer and drove us from our home !
Some of our people plead with them, our country to retain,
While others did contest our rights with arms, but all in vain.
With sorrow, grief and suffering, we were forced at last to go,
From the graves of our forefathers to a land we did not know.
But this was now guaranteed to us, " as long as water shall run,"
Yet on they pushed us, on and on toward the setting sun !

" And this will be the last move," they tell us, if we go;
" You will hold the country this time as long as grass shall grow,
" For the good,Great Father's promise is a very sacred pledge,
" And to all his children does he give the greatest privilege ;"
That is to all children he adopts from every race of man,
Except the rightful owners of this broad and bounteous land !
They must in meek submission bow unto the hand of might,
To them the courts of law are barred, they can make no legal fight!

If the Indian seeks the Government, there his grievance to relate,
He must first obtain permission from those who rule the State !
If his rights are there denied him and an attorney he would seek,
He is sternly then reminded he has no right to speak !
" For under section so and so, which guides your legal move,
" You see no attorneys can appear for you, except if we approve ;
" And if, in our opinion, your el aim does not adhere
" To the interests of the public, then your cause we cannot hear."

" This is a Christian Nation," they oft with pride maintain,
And even on their money their faith they do proclaim.
And none can hold an office here in this Christian land,
Unless he believes in Heaven and the future state of man ;
In every town are churches, God's word is everywhere,
E'en legislation, good or bad, begins each day with prayer,
" This is the home of freedom, where justice rules the land !
" And all (save Indian people) their rights may here demand !"

The foreigner from Europe's shore or the ignorant African
Has the right to sit in Congress' halls and legislation plan !
Turning the treaty records o'er, in the first that comes to view,
I see this gracious Government guaranteed these rights to you,
And why you're treated as children, or ruled with an iron hand,
Nor allowed to be politically free, is more than I understand,
Unless it be " in Heaven you are to find your treasures dear,"
And your pious Christian teachers are to take " their treasures " here.

But I do not blame the Christians, if Christians true they be,
And it's not their Bible teachings that bring such grief to thee ;
It is not the faith that men believe, it is the deeds they do,
That sometimes hurt their fellowmen and probe their conscience, too.
If " we are all children of one God," are we not equal here ?
Are not the Indian's liberties and rights, to Him as dear ?
If we an earnest effort make, our rights here to obtain,
Then, perhaps with His assistance, that privilege we shall gain.

I believe the American people are just and kind and true,
They would fight for our protection, if our grievance they but knew.
True, some with selfish motives would keep us still suppressed,
But the great controlling public would strive to do what is best.
And none has their attention called to our sad, humiliated state,
Or quickly would they all demand that Congress reparation make.
So the fault with us has partly been, because we don't complain,
But allow ourselves thus to be robbed for selfish plotters' gain !

Why should we be a separate people, the target of every man ?
We, who owned this country once, should be right in the van.
No one would objections raise and surely Congress can
Declare all Indians vested with the rights of every man.
And grant us prompt permission to prove our every claim,
And pay us the obligations the Government has made in vain ;
Then to our oppressors will we prove, who deny our right to live,
That Indians will make good citizens, if to them a chance you give.

Yours Sincerely

Richard C. Adams,

Representing the Delaware Indians.